LINE by LINE

STORIES FOR LEARNERS OF ENGLISH

SECOND EDITION

BEGINNING

Steven J. Molinsky / Bill Bliss

PRENTICE HALL REGENTS
Englewood Cliffs, New Jersey 07632

Library of Congress Cataloging-in-Publication Data

Molinsky, Steven J.
    Line by line stories for learners of English : beginning /
Steven J. Molinsky, Bill Bliss.—2nd ed.
        pp. 128
        "Line by line : beginning consists of the reading selections and
accompanying exercises contained in Side by side, second edition:
books 1 and 2"—P. 111.
        ISBN 0-13-536871-5
        1. English language—Textbooks for foreign speakers.   I. Bliss,
Bill.   II. Molinsky, Steven J. Side by side.   III. Title.
PE1128.M68   1990
428.2′4—dc20   89-37126
                                                    CIP

Editorial/production supervision: Noël Vreeland Carter
Art supervision: Meg Van Arsdale
Manufacturing buyer: Peter Havens
Cover design: Karen Stephens

Illustrated by Richard E. Hill

 © 1990 by Prentice-Hall, Inc.
A Division of Simon & Schuster
Englewood Cliffs, New Jersey 07632

Printed in the United States of America

10   9   8   7   6   5   4   3   2

ISBN 0-13-536871-5

Prentice-Hall International (UK) Limited, *London*
Prentice-Hall of Australia Pty. Limited, *Sydney*
Prentice-Hall Canada Inc., *Toronto*
Prentice-Hall Hispanoamericana, S.A., *Mexico*
Prentice-Hall of India Private Limited, *New Delhi*
Prentice-Hall of Japan, Inc., *Tokyo*
Simon & Schuster Asia Pte. Ltd., *Singapore*
Editora Prentice-Hall do Brasil, Ltda., *Rio de Janeiro*

To the Teacher

Line by Line: Beginning consists of the reading selections and accompanying exercises contained in *Side by Side Second Edition: Books 1 and 2*. It is designed to serve as a supplementary or stand-alone reader.

The goal of *Line by Line* is to provide meaningful, relevant, and enjoyable reading practice while offering a clear, intensive focus on specific aspects of English grammar. The readings depict a wide range of characters and everyday life situations—many dealing with key adult lifeskill competencies, such as food, employment, health, housing, shopping, and transportation.

AN OVERVIEW

Chapter Opening Pages

The opening page of each chapter provides an overview of the grammatical structures treated in the chapter.

Reading Selections

Short reading selections offer enjoyable reading practice that simultaneously reinforces specific grammatical structures. Accompanying illustrations serve as visual cues that guide learners through the reading, helping to clarify both context and new vocabulary.

Check-Up

Check-Up exercises provide focused practice in reading comprehension and vocabulary development. Also, listening exercises enable students to develop their aural comprehension skills through a variety of listening activities.

How About You?

How About You? activities are intended to provide students with opportunities to apply lesson content to their own lives and experiences and to share opinions in class.

In Your Own words

These activities provide topics and themes for student compositions and classroom discussions. Students write about their friends, families, homes, schools, jobs, and themselves.

SUGGESTED TEACHING STRATEGIES

Introducing Reading Selections

You may wish to preview each story either by briefly setting the scene or by having students talk about the illustrations or predict the content of the story from the title. You may also find it useful to introduce beforehand any vocabulary you think your students might be unfamiliar with. On the other hand, you may prefer to skip the previewing step, and instead have students experience the subject matter and any unfamiliar words in the context of the initial reading of the story.

There are many ways in which students can read and talk about the stories. Students may read silently to themselves or follow along as the story is read by you, by one or more students, or on the tape. You should then ask students if they have any questions and check understanding of vocabulary.

Q & A Exercises

Q & A exercises are included as part of the Check-Up after many of the reading selections. These exercises are designed to give students conversation practice based on information contained in the stories. Italic type is used in the Q & A model to highlight which words get replaced by different information contained in the reading.

Call on a pair of students to present the Q & A model. Have students work in pairs to create new dialogs based on the model, and then call on pairs to present their new dialogs to the class.

In Your Own Words

These activities are designed to guide students in their creation of original stories. Students are asked to write about topics such as their homes, schools, friends, families, and themselves.

You should go over the instructions for the activities and make sure students understand what is expected. Students should then write their stories, taking sufficient time to think about what they want to say, using a dictionary for any new words they wish to include. These activities are perhaps most appropriately assigned for homework to guarantee that all students will have sufficient time to develop their ideas and write them out.

Many teachers will find these written pieces a basis for effective peer work in class. Students can work together, telling their stories to each other, asking and answering questions about the stories, and correcting each other's written work.

As a final step, the *In Your Own Words* activities serve as a vehicle for classroom speaking practice. Students can tell their own stories, or perhaps tell the stories of their "peer-work" partners, while the rest of the class listens and asks questions.

In conclusion, we have attempted to help students develop their reading and writing abilities in English through a collection of carefully structured stories that are both lighthearted in content and relevant to students' lives. While we hope that we have conveyed to you the substance of our textbook, we also hope that we have conveyed the spirit: that the study of reading and writing can be dynamic . . . communicative . . . and fun!

Steven J. Molinsky
Bill Bliss

Contents

To Be: Introduction

What's Your Name?

WHAT'S YOUR NAME?

My name is David Miller. I'm American. I'm from New York.

My name is Mrs. White. My phone number is 237–5976.

My name is Susan Black. My address is 378 Main Street, Waterville, Florida. My license number is 112897.

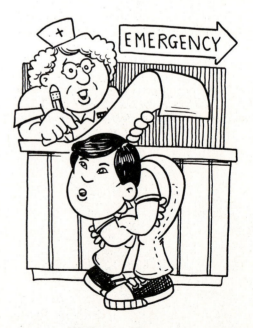

My name is Mr. Taylor. My apartment number is 3–B.

My name is William Chen. My address is 694 River Street, Brooklyn, New York. My telephone number is 469–7750. My Social Security number is 044-35-9862.

✔ CHECK-UP

Match

_____ 1. name

_____ 2. address

_____ 3. phone number

_____ 4. apartment number

_____ 5. Social Security number

a. 237–5976

b. 3–B

c. William Chen

d. 044-35-9862

e. 378 Main Street

Listening

Listen and choose the best answer.

1. a. Mrs. White
    b. Susan Miller

2. a. 394 Main Street
    b. 394 River Street

3. a. 9–D
    b. 9–B

4. a. 748–2066
    b. 748–2260

5. a. 060-83-8752
    b. 060-83-8275

✏ IN YOUR OWN WORDS

Fill out the form.

ACME COMPANY
Employment Application Form

Name _____

Address _____

_____

Telephone Number _____

Social Security Number _____

To Be + Location
Subject Pronouns

The Students in My English Class

All the Students in My English Class Are Absent Today

THE STUDENTS IN MY ENGLISH CLASS

The students in my English class are very interesting. Henry is Chinese. He's from Shanghai. Natasha is Russian. She's from Leningrad. Mr. and Mrs. Ramirez are Puerto Rican. They're from San Juan.

George is Greek. He's from Athens. Nicole is French. She's from Paris. Mr. and Mrs. Sato are Japanese. They're from Tokyo. My friend Maria and I are Mexican. We're from Mexico City.

Yes, the students in my English class are very interesting. We're from many different countries . . . and we're friends.

✓CHECK-UP

True or False?

1. Nicole is Greek.
2. Natasha is Russian.
3. Henry is from Mexico City.
4. Mr. Sato is from Tokyo.
5. Mrs. Ramirez is Chinese.
6. The students in the class are from many countries.

How about YOU?

Tell about the students in YOUR English class. Where are they from?

READING

ALL THE STUDENTS IN MY ENGLISH CLASS ARE ABSENT TODAY

All the students in my English class are absent today. George is absent. He's in the hospital. Maria is absent. She's at the dentist. Mr. and Mrs. Sato are absent. They're at the Social Security office. Even our English teacher is absent. He's home in bed!

What a shame! Everybody in my English class is absent today. Everybody except me.

✓ CHECK-UP

Answer These Questions

1. Where's George?
2. Where's Maria?
3. Where are Mr. and Mrs. Sato?
4. Where's the English teacher?

Listening

Listen and choose the best answer.

1. a. bank   b. park
2. a. hospital   b. library
3. a. He's   b. She's
4. a. He's   b. She's
5. a. We're   b. They're
6. a. We're   b. They're

How about YOU?

Tell about YOUR English class:
   Which students are in class today?
   Which students are absent today?
   Where are they?

7

Present Continuous Tense

In the Park

At Home in the Yard

IN THE PARK

The Jones family is in the park today. The sun is shining and the birds are singing. It's a beautiful day!

Mr. Jones is reading the newspaper. Mrs. Jones is listening to the radio. Sally and Patty Jones are studying. And Tommy Jones is playing the guitar.

The Jones family is very happy today. It's a beautiful day and they're in the park.

AT HOME IN THE YARD

The Smith family is at home in the yard today. The sun is shining and the birds are singing. It's a beautiful day!

Mr. Smith is planting flowers. Mrs. Smith is drinking lemonade and reading a book. Mary and Billy Smith are playing with the dog. And Sam Smith is sleeping.

The Smith family is very happy today. It's a beautiful day and they're at home in the yard.

✔CHECK-UP

True or False?

1. The Jones family is at home in the yard today.
2. Mr. Smith is planting flowers.
3. Sally Jones is studying.
4. Billy Smith is reading a book.
5. The Smith family is singing.
6. The Jones family and the Smith family are very happy today.

Listening

Listen and choose the best answer.

1. a. She's reading.
   b. I'm reading.

2. a. He's cooking.
   b. She's cooking.

3. a. He's watching TV.
   b. She's watching TV.

Q & A

Using this model, make questions and answers based on the stories on page 10.

A. What's *Mr. Jones* doing?
B. *He's reading the newspaper.*

4. a. We're studying.
   b. They're studying.

5. a. We're eating.
   b. They're eating.

6. a. You're drinking lemonade.
   b. We're drinking lemonade.

✎IN YOUR OWN WORDS

For Writing and Discussion

AT THE BEACH

The Martinez family is at the beach today. Using this picture, tell a story about the Martinez family.

Possessive Adjectives

A Busy Day

A BUSY DAY

Everybody at 149 River Street is very busy today. Mr. Anderson is cleaning his kitchen. Mrs. Wilson is fixing her kitchen sink. Mr. and Mrs. Thomas are painting their living room. Mrs. Black is doing her exercises. Tommy Lee is feeding his dog. And Mr. and Mrs. Lane are washing their car.

I'm busy, too. I'm washing my windows . . . and of course, I'm watching all my neighbors. It's a very busy day at 149 River Street.

✔CHECK-UP

True or False?

1. Mr. Anderson is in his kitchen.
2. Tommy is eating.
3. Mr. and Mrs. Lane are in their apartment.
4. Mrs. Thomas is painting.
5. Their address is 147 River Street.

Q & A

Using this model, make questions and answers based on the story.

   A. What's *Mr. Anderson* doing?
   B. *He's cleaning his kitchen.*

Listening

Listen and choose the best answer.

1. a. My kitchen.
   b. My homework.

2. a. The piano.
   b. Lemonade.

3. a. The newspaper.
   b. Dinner.

4. a. A book.
   b. Breakfast.

5. a. TV.
   b. His clothes.

6. a. My windows.
   b. The birds.

IN YOUR OWN WORDS

For Writing and Discussion

A BUSY DAY

Everybody at 210 Main Street is very busy today. Using the picture, tell a story about them.

Adjectives

Dear Mother

DEAR MOTHER

Royal Sludge Hotel

Dear Mother,

I'm writing to you from our hotel at Sludge Beach. Ralph and I are on vacation with the children for a few days. We're happy to be here, but to tell the truth, we're having a few problems.

The weather isn't very good. In fact, it's cold and cloudy. Right now I'm looking out the window and it's raining cats and dogs.

The children aren't very happy. In fact, they're bored and they're having a terrible time. Right now they're sitting on the bed, playing cards and watching TV.

The restaurants here are expensive, and the food isn't very good. In fact, Ralph is at the doctor's office right now. He's having problems with his stomach.

All the other hotels here are beautiful and new. Our hotel is ugly, and it's very, very old. In fact, right now a repairman is fixing the toilet.

As you can see, Mother, we're having a few problems here at Sludge Beach, but we're happy. We're happy to be on vacation, and we're happy to be together.

See you soon.

Love,
Ethel

✔CHECK-UP

True or False?

1. The weather is beautiful.
2. The children are swimming.
3. Their hotel is old.
4. A repairman is fixing the window.
5. Ralph isn't at the hotel right now.
6. Ethel is watching the cats and dogs.

Listening

Listen and choose the best answer.

1. a. It's old.   b. It's sunny.
2. a. It's small.   b. It's bored.
3. a. They're noisy.   b. They're new.
4. a. He's cloudy.   b. He's handsome.
5. a. It's large.   b. It's fat.
6. a. It's easy.   b. It's beautiful.

To Be: Review
Present Continuous Tense: Review
Prepositions of Location

Arthur Is Very Angry

Tom's Wedding Day

READING

ARTHUR IS VERY ANGRY

It's late at night. Arthur is sitting on his bed and he's looking at his clock. His neighbors are making a lot of noise, and Arthur is VERY angry.

The people in Apartment 2 are dancing. The man in Apartment 3 is vacuuming the carpet in his living room. The woman in Apartment 4 is practicing the violin. The teenagers in Apartment 5 are listening to loud rock music. The dog in Apartment 6 is barking. And the people in Apartment 7 are having a big argument.

It's very late and Arthur is tired and angry. What a terrible night!

✔ CHECK-UP

Q & A

Using this model, make questions and answers based on the story.

A. What's *the man in Apartment 3* doing?
B. *He's vacuuming the carpet in his living room.*

Choose

1. Arthur's neighbors are
   a. noisy.
   b. angry.

2. The man in Apartment 3 is
   a. painting his apartment.
   b. cleaning his apartment.

3. The noisy people in Apartment 5 are
   a. young.
   b. old.

4. The dog in Apartment 6 isn't
   a. sleeping.
   b. making noise.

5. The woman in Apartment 4 is
   a. playing cards.
   b. playing music.

6. Arthur isn't very
   a. happy.
   b. tired.

TOM'S WEDDING DAY

Today is a very special day. It's my wedding day, and all my family and friends are here. Everybody is having a wonderful time.

My wife, Jane, is standing in front of the fireplace. She's wearing a beautiful white wedding gown. Uncle Harry is taking her photograph, and Aunt Emma is crying. (She's very sentimental.)

The band is playing my favorite popular music. My mother is dancing with Jane's father, and Jane's mother is dancing with my father.

My sister and Jane's brother are standing in the yard, eating wedding cake and talking about politics. Our grandparents are sitting in the corner, drinking champagne and talking about "the good old days."

Everybody is having a good time. People are singing, dancing, and laughing, and our families are getting to know each other. It's a very special day.

✓ CHECK-UP

Answer These Questions

1. Where is Jane standing?
2. What's she wearing?
3. What's Uncle Harry doing?
4. What's Aunt Emma doing?
5. What are Tom's sister and Jane's brother doing?
6. What are their grandparents doing?

Listening: *Quiet or Noisy?*

Listen to the sentence. Are the people quiet or noisy?

1. a. quiet   b. noisy
2. a. quiet   b. noisy
3. a. quiet   b. noisy
4. a. quiet   b. noisy
5. a. quiet   b. noisy
6. a. quiet   b. noisy

✏ IN YOUR OWN WORDS

For Writing and Discussion

JENNIFER'S BIRTHDAY PARTY

Today is a very special day. It's Jennifer's birthday party, and all her family and friends are there. Using this picture, tell a story about her party.

7

Prepositions
There Is/There Are

The New Shopping Mall

Jane's Apartment Building

THE NEW SHOPPING MALL

Everybody in Brewster is talking about the city's new shopping mall. The mall is outside the city, next to the Brewster airport. There are more than one hundred stores in the mall.

There are two big department stores. There are many clothing stores for men, women, and children. There's a very big toy store. There are two shoe stores, two drug stores, and four restaurants. There's even a movie theater.

Almost all the people in Brewster are happy that their city's new shopping mall is now open. But some people aren't happy. The owners of the small stores in the old center of town are very upset. They're upset because there aren't many people shopping in their stores in the center of town. They're all shopping at the new mall.

✓ CHECK-UP

Choose

1. Everybody in Brewster is
   a. at the airport.
   b. outside the city.
   c. talking about the mall.

2. In the mall, there are
   a. two toy stores.
   b. two drug stores.
   c. two restaurants.

3. In the mall,
   a. there are toy stores and shoe stores.
   b. there are restaurants and drug stores.
   c. there are clothing stores and movie theaters.

4. The store owners in the center of town are upset because
   a. people aren't shopping in their stores.
   b. people aren't shopping at the mall.
   c. they're very old.

How about YOU?

Is there a shopping mall in your city or town? Are there small stores in your city or town? Tell about the stores where you live.

READING

JANE'S APARTMENT BUILDING

Jane's apartment building is in the center of town. Jane is very happy there because the building is in a very convenient place.

Across from the building, there's a laundromat, a bank, and a post office. Next to the building, there's a drug store and a restaurant. Around the corner from the building, there are two gas stations.

There's a lot of noise near Jane's apartment building. There are a lot of cars on the street, and there are a lot of people walking on the sidewalk all day and all night.

Jane isn't very upset about the noise, though. Her building is in the center of town. It's a very busy place, but for Jane, it's a very convenient place to live.

✓ CHECK-UP

Answer These Questions

1. Where is Jane's apartment building?
2. What's across from her building?
3. Is there a drug store near her building?
4. Why is there a lot of noise near Jane's building?
5. Why is Jane happy there?

True or False?

1. Jane's apartment is in a very convenient place.
2. There's a laundromat around the corner from her building.
3. Two gas stations are nearby.
4. There are a lot of cars on the sidewalk.
5. The center of town is very noisy.

Listening

What words do you hear?

Example	ⓐ park	b. shoe store	ⓒ drug store
1.	a. park	b. bank	c. restaurant
2.	a. police station	b. gas station	c. fire station
3.	a. supermarket	b. department store	c. school
4.	a. toy store	b. two toy stores	c. movie theater
5.	a. bank	b. clothing store	c. shoe store

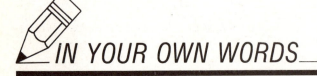

IN YOUR OWN WORDS

For Writing and Discussion

GEORGE'S APARTMENT BUILDING

George's apartment building is in the center of town. George is very happy there because the building is in a very convenient place. Using the picture, tell about George's neighborhood.

How about YOU?

Tell about YOUR neighborhood:
  Is it convenient? Is it very busy?
  Is it noisy or quiet?

8

Singular/Plural
Adjectives

Nothing to Wear

Christmas Shopping

NOTHING TO WEAR

Fred is upset this morning. He's looking for something to wear to work, but there's nothing in his closet.

He's looking for a clean shirt, but all his shirts are dirty. He's looking for a sports jacket, but all his sports jackets are at the dry cleaner's. He's looking for a pair of pants, but all the pants in his closet are ripped. And he's looking for a pair of socks, but all his socks are on the clothesline, and it's raining!

Fred is having a difficult time this morning. He's getting dressed for work, but his closet is empty and there's nothing to wear.

✔CHECK-UP

Choose

1. Fred's closet is
   a. upset.
   b. empty.

2. Fred is
   a. at home.
   b. at work.

3. Fred's shirts are
   a. dirty.
   b. clean.

4. He's looking for a pair of
   a. jackets.
   b. pants.

5. The weather is
   a. not very good.
   b. beautiful.

6. Fred is upset because
   a. he's getting dressed.
   b. there's nothing to wear.

Choose

What word *doesn't* belong?

1. a. shoes	b. socks	c. earrings	d. boots
2. a. necklace	b. bracelet	c. sweater	d. earring
3. a. skirt	b. raincoat	c. jacket	d. coat
4. a. dress	b. blouse	c. skirt	d. tie
5. a. umbrella	b. shirt	c. briefcase	d. purse

CHRISTMAS SHOPPING

Mrs. Johnson is doing her Christmas shopping. She's looking for Christmas gifts for her family, but she's having a lot of trouble.

She's looking for a brown briefcase for her husband, but all the briefcases are black. She's looking for a plain tie for her brother, but all the ties are striped. She's looking for a cotton blouse for her daughter, but all the blouses are polyester.

She's looking for an inexpensive necklace for her sister, but all the necklaces are expensive. She's looking for a gray or brown raincoat for her father-in-law, but all the raincoats are yellow. And she's looking for a leather purse for her mother-in-law, but all the purses are vinyl.

Poor Mrs. Johnson is very frustrated. She's looking for special gifts for all the special people in her family, but she's having a lot of trouble.

Good luck with your Christmas shopping, Mrs. Johnson! And Merry Christmas!

✓CHECK-UP

Q & A

Mrs. Johnson is in the department store. Using this model, create dialogs based on the story.

A. Excuse me. I'm looking for *a brown briefcase* for *my husband*.
B. I'm sorry. All our *briefcases* are *black*.

Listening

Listen and choose the word you hear.

1. a. tie   b. ties
2. a. jacket   b. jackets
3. a. blouse   b. blouses
4. a. sock   b. socks
5. a. boot   b. boots
6. a. umbrella   b. umbrellas

9

Simple Present Tense
Mr. and Mrs. DiCarlo

MR. AND MRS. DiCARLO

Mr. and Mrs. DiCarlo live in an old Italian neighborhood in New York City. They speak a little English, but usually they speak Italian.

They read the Italian newspaper. They listen to Italian radio programs. They shop at the Italian grocery store around the corner from their apartment building. And every day they visit their friends and neighbors and talk about life back in "the old country."

Mr. and Mrs. DiCarlo are upset about their son, Joe. He lives in a small suburb outside the city, and he speaks very little Italian. He reads American newspapers. He listens to American radio programs. He shops at big suburban supermarkets and shopping malls. And when he visits his friends and neighbors, he speaks only English.

In fact, the only time Joe speaks Italian is when he calls Mr. and Mrs. DiCarlo on the telephone or when he visits every weekend.

Mr. and Mrs. DiCarlo are sad because their son speaks so little Italian. They're afraid he's forgetting his language, his culture, and his country.

☑ CHECK-UP

Answer These Questions

1. Where do Mr. and Mrs. DiCarlo live?
2. Where does Joe live?
3. How much English do Mr. and Mrs. DiCarlo speak?
4. How much Italian does Joe speak?
5. What do Mr. and Mrs. DiCarlo read?
6. What does Joe read?
7. What do Mr. and Mrs. DiCarlo listen to?
8. What does Joe listen to?
9. Where do Mr. and Mrs. DiCarlo shop?
10. Where does Joe shop?

What's the Word?

1. Mr. DiCarlo _____ a little English.
2. Mrs. DiCarlo _____ at the grocery store.
3. They _____ the Italian newspaper every day.
4. Joe _____ outside the city.
5. He _____ American radio programs.
6. His friends _____ only English.
7. Mrs. DiCarlo _____ her neighbors every day.
8. She _____ about life in "the old country."
9. Their friends _____ in New York City.
10. They _____ their friends on the telephone.

Choose

What word *doesn't* belong?

1. a. coffee   b. newspaper   c. tea   d. wine
2. a. French   b. Spanish   c. Rome   d. German
3. a. Italian   b. Russian   c. Japanese   d. New York
4. a. mall   b. supermarket   c. neighborhood   d. store
5. a. son   b. friend   c. neighbor   d. landlord
6. a. lunch   b. dinner   c. food   d. restaurant

Listening

Listen and choose the best answer.

1. a. The newspaper.   b. Mexican food.
2. a. The newspaper.   b. Mexican food.
3. a. Their clothes.   b. TV.
4. a. Their clothes.   b. TV.
5. a. Songs.   b. Coffee.
6. a. Songs.   b. Coffee.

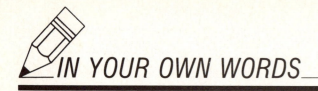

IN YOUR OWN WORDS

For Writing and Discussion

MRS. KOWALSKI

Mrs. Kowalski lives in an old Polish neighborhood in Chicago. She's upset about her son, Michael, and his wife, Kathy. Using the story on page 75 as a model, tell a story about Mrs. Kowalski.

Tell about yourself:
    What do you do every day?
    Who do you visit?
    What do you talk about?

Now, tell about another person (a friend, someone in your family, or another student in your class):
    What does he/she do every day?
    Who does he/she visit?
    What does he/she talk about?

Simple Present Tense:
Yes/No Questions
Negatives
Short Answers

Every Weekend Is Important to the Franklin Family

A Very Outgoing Person

EVERY WEEKEND IS IMPORTANT TO THE FRANKLIN FAMILY

Every weekend is important to the Franklin family. During the week they don't have very much time together, but they spend A LOT of time together on the weekend.

Mr. Franklin works at the shoe store downtown during the week, but he doesn't work there on the weekend. Mrs. Franklin works at the city hospital during the week, but she doesn't work there on the weekend. Bobby and Sally Franklin go to the elementary school during the week, but they don't go there on the weekend. And the Franklin's dog, Rover, stays home alone during the week, but he doesn't stay home alone on the weekend.

On Saturday and Sunday the Franklins spend their time together. On Saturday morning they clean the house together. On Saturday afternoon they work in the garden together. And on Saturday evening they sit in the living room and watch TV together. On Sunday morning they go to church together. On Sunday afternoon they have a big dinner together. And on Sunday evening they play their musical instruments together.

As you can see, every weekend is special to the Franklins. It's their only time together as a family.

Q & A

Using these models, make questions and answers based on the story on page 84.

A. What *does Mr. Franklin* do during the week?
B. *He works at the shoe store downtown.*

A. What do the Franklins do on *Saturday morning?*
B. They *clean the house* together.

Do or Does?

1. What kind of food _____ you like?
2. _____ Mr. Franklin go to Stanley's Restaurant?
3. _____ you speak Spanish?
4. When _____ Bobby go to school?
5. _____ she work downtown?
6. Where _____ they live?

Listening

Choose the best answer to finish the sentence.

1. a. you do.   b. they do.
2. a. he does.   b. he doesn't.
3. a. I do.   b. he does.
4. a. she does.   b. we do.
5. a. they don't.   b. we don't.
6. a. she does.   b. she doesn't.
7. a. I do.   b. I don't.
8. a. he doesn't.   b. she doesn't.

Answer These Questions

1. Does Mr. Franklin work at the shoe store?
2. Do Bobby and Sally go to school during the week?
3. Does Mrs. Franklin work at the shoe store?
4. Do Mr. and Mrs. Franklin have much time together during the week?
5. Does Sally Franklin watch TV on Saturday evening?
6. Do Sally and her brother clean the house on Saturday morning?
7. Does Mr. Franklin work in the garden on Saturday evening?

Don't or Doesn't?

1. My husband _____ like international food.
2. I _____ like coffee.
3. They _____ play musical instruments.
4. Mrs. Wilson _____ shop at the mall.
5. My sister and I _____ watch TV during the week.
6. Our dog _____ like our neighbor's cat.

A VERY OUTGOING PERSON

Alice is a very outgoing person. She spends a lot of time with her friends. She goes to parties. She goes to movies. And she goes to night clubs. She's very popular.

She also likes sports very much. She plays basketball. She plays baseball. And she plays volleyball. She's very athletic.

Alice doesn't stay home alone very often. She doesn't read many books. She doesn't watch TV. And she doesn't listen to music. She's very active.

As you can see, Alice is a very outgoing person.

IN YOUR OWN WORDS

For Writing and Discussion

A VERY SHY PERSON

Using the story about Alice as a model, tell a story about Sheldon. Begin your story:

Sheldon is a very shy person. He doesn't spend a lot of time with his friends. He doesn't go . . .

How about YOU?

Tell about yourself:
　　What kind of person are you?
　　Are you outgoing? Are you shy?
　　Tell how you spend your time.

Object Pronouns
Simple Present Tense:
s vs. non-s Endings
Adverbs of Frequency

Close Friends

CLOSE FRIENDS

My husband and I are very lucky. We have many close friends in this city, and they're all interesting people.

Our friend Greta is an actress. We see her when she isn't making a movie in Hollywood. When we get together with her, she always tells us about her life in Hollywood as a movie star. Greta is a very close friend. We like her very much.

Our friend Dan is a scientist. We see him when he isn't busy in his laboratory. When we get together with him, he always tells us about his new experiments. Dan is a very close friend. We like him very much.

Our friends Bob and Carol are famous newspaper reporters. We see them when they aren't traveling around the world. When we get together with them, they always tell us about their conversations with presidents and prime ministers. Bob and Carol are very close friends. We like them very much.

Unfortunately, we don't see Greta, Dan, Bob, and Carol very often. In fact, we rarely see them because they're usually so busy. But we think about them all the time.

What's the Word?

Dan is always busy. _____ works in _____ laboratory every day. Dan's friends rarely see
         1   2
_____. When they see _____, _____ usually talks about _____ experiments. Everybody
3   4   5   6
likes _____ very much. _____ is a very nice person.
      7   8

Greta is a famous actress. _____ lives in Hollywood. _____ movies are very popular.
                      9   10
When _____ walks down the street, people always say "hello" to _____ and tell _____ how
      11   12   13
much they like _____ movies.
              14

Bob and Carol are reporters. _____ friends don't see _____ very often because _____
                    15   16   17
travel around the world all the time. Presidents and prime ministers often call _____ on the
                                            18
telephone. _____ like _____ work very much.
          19   20

Listening

Who and what are they talking about?

1. a. daughter
   b. son

2. a. window
   b. windows

3. a. grandfather
   b. aunt

4. a. sink
   b. toilets

5. a. Mr. Jones
   b. Mr. and Mrs. Jones

6. a. Mr. Green
   b. Mr. and Mrs. Green

IN YOUR OWN WORDS

For Writing and Discussion

MY CLOSE FRIENDS

Tell about your close friends.

What are their names?
Where do they live?
What do they do?
When do you get together with them?
What do you talk about?

THE ACE EMPLOYMENT SERVICE

   Roy, Susan, Lana, and Tina are sitting in the reception room at the Ace Employment Service. They're all looking for work, and they're hoping they can find jobs today.

   Roy is looking for a job as a superintendent. He can paint walls. He can fix motors. And he can repair locks. Susan is looking for a job as a secretary. She can type. She can file. And she can speak well on the telephone. Lana and Tina are looking for jobs as actresses. They can sing. They can dance. And they can act.

   Good luck, Roy! Good luck, Susan! Good luck, Lana and Tina! We hope you can find the jobs you're looking for.

Q & A

Roy, Susan, Lana, and Tina are having their interviews at the Ace Employment Service. Using this model, create dialogs based on the story.

A. What's your name?
B. *Roy Smith.*
A. Nice to meet you. Tell me, *Roy,* what kind of job are you looking for?
B. I'm looking for a job as a *superintendent.*
A. What can you do?
B. I can *paint walls, fix motors,* and *repair locks.*

Listening

Can or Can't?

Listen and circle.

1. a. can   b. can't
2. a. can   b. can't
3. a. can   b. can't
4. a. can   b. can't
5. a. can   b. can't
6. a. can   b. can't

What Can They Do?

Choose what each person can do.

1. a. sing   b. dance
2. a. file   b. type
3. a. fix motors   b. repair locks
4. a. cook   b. bake
5. a. drive a truck b. drive a bus
6. a. teach history b. teach science

APPLYING FOR A DRIVER'S LICENSE

Henry is annoyed. He's applying for a driver's license, and he's upset about all the things he has to do.

First, he has to go to the Motor Vehicles Department and pick up an application form. He can't ask for the form by telephone, and he can't ask for it by mail. He has to go downtown and pick up the form in person.

He has to fill out the form in duplicate. He can't use a pencil. He has to use a pen. He can't use blue ink. He has to use black ink. And he can't write in script. He has to print.

He also has to attach two photographs to the application. They can't be old photographs. They have to be new. They can't be large. They have to be small. And they can't be black and white. They have to be color.

Then he has to submit his application. He has to wait in a long line to pay his application fee. He has to wait in another long line to have an eye examination. And believe it or not, he has to wait in ANOTHER long line to take a written test!

Finally, he has to take a road test. He has to start the car. He has to make a right turn, a left turn, and a U-turn. And he even has to park his car on a crowded city street.

No wonder Henry is annoyed! He's applying for his driver's license, and he can't believe all the things he has to do.

☑CHECK-UP

Answer These Questions

1. Can Henry apply for a driver's license by mail?
2. Where does he have to go to apply for a license?
3. How many photographs does he have to attach to the application?
4. Can Henry use black and white photographs?
5. What does he have to do during the road test?

Fix This Sign

This sign at the Motor Vehicles Department is wrong. The things people have to do are in the wrong order. On a separate sheet of paper, fix the sign based on the story.

How to Apply for a Driver's License

Have an eye examination.
Pay the application fee.
Take a road test.
Pick up an application form.
Take a written test.
Fill out the form in duplicate.

IN YOUR OWN WORDS

For Writing and Discussion

Explain how to apply for one of the following: a passport, a marriage license, a loan, or something else. In your explanation, use "You have to."*

*"You have to" = "A person has to"

14

Future: Going to
Time Expressions

Happy New Year!

The Fortune Teller

READING

HAPPY NEW YEAR!

It's December thirty-first, New Year's Eve. Bob and Sally Simpson are celebrating the holiday with their children, Lucy and Tom. The Simpsons are a very happy family this New Year's Eve. Next year is going to be a very good year for the entire family.

Next year, Bob and Sally are going to take a long vacation. They're going to visit Sally's cousin in California. Lucy is going to finish high school. She's going to move to Boston and begin college. Tom is going to get his driver's license. He's going to save a lot of money and buy a used car.

As you can see, the Simpsons are really looking forward to next year. It's going to be a happy year for all of them.

Happy New Year!

✓ CHECK-UP

Complete the Conversation

Fill in the missing words and practice the dialog with another student.

A. Lucy, _____ do next year?
₁

B. _____ begin college.
₂

A. And your brother? _____ do next year?
₃

B. _____ get his driver's license.
₄

A. How about your parents? _____ do next year?
₅

B. _____ take a long vacation.
₆

A. Well, Happy New Year, Lucy!

B. Happy New Year!

Listening

Listen and choose the words you hear.

1. a. Next month.   b. Next Monday.
2. a. This Sunday.   b. This summer.
3. a. Tomorrow afternoon.   b. This afternoon.
4. a. Next November.   b. Next December.
5. a. Next year.   b. Next week.

6. a. This evening.   b. This morning.
7. a. This Tuesday.   b. This Thursday.
8. a. Next winter.   b. Next summer.
9. a. Tomorrow.   b. This March.
10. a. This month.   b. At once.

THE FORTUNE TELLER

Walter is visiting Madame Sophia, the famous fortune teller. He's very concerned about his future, and Madame Sophia is telling him what is going to happen next year. According to Madame Sophia, next year is going to be a very interesting year in Walter's life.

In January he's going to meet a very nice woman and fall in love.

In February he's going to get married.

In March he's going to take a trip to a warm, sunny place.

In April he's going to have a bad cold.

In May his parents are going to move to a beautiful city in California.

In June there's going to be a fire in his apartment building, and he's going to have to find a new place to live.

In July his friends are going to give him a radio for his birthday.

In August his boss is going to fire him.

In September he's going to start a new job with a very big salary.

In October he's going to be in a car accident, but he isn't going to be hurt.

In November he's going to be on a television game show and win a new car.

And in December he's going to become a father!

According to Madame Sophia, a lot is certainly going to happen in Walter's life next year. But Walter isn't sure he believes any of this. He doesn't believe in fortunes or fortune tellers. But in January he's going to get a haircut and buy a lot of new clothes, just in case Madame Sophia is right and he meets a wonderful woman and falls in love!

 **CHECK-UP**

Q & A

Walter is talking to Madame Sophia. Using these models, create dialogs based on the story.

A. Tell me, what's going to happen in *January?*
B. In *January?* Oh, . . . *January* is going to be a very good month.
A. Really? What's going to happen?
B. *You're going to meet a very nice woman and fall in love.*
A. Oh! That's wonderful!

A. Tell me, what's going to happen in *April?*
B. In *April?* Oh, . . . *April* is going to be a very bad month.
A. Really? What's going to happen?
B. *You're going to have a bad cold.*
A. Oh! That's terrible!

15

Past Tense: Regular Verbs Introduction to Irregular Verbs

The Wilsons' Party

THE WILSONS' PARTY

Mr. and Mrs. Wilson invited all their friends and neighbors to a party last night. They stayed home all day yesterday and prepared for the party.

In the morning the Wilsons worked outside. Their daughter, Margaret, cleaned the yard. Their son, Bob, painted the fence. Mrs. Wilson planted flowers in the garden, and Mr. Wilson fixed their broken front steps.

In the afternoon the Wilsons worked inside the house. Margaret washed the floors and vacuumed the living room carpet. Bob dusted the furniture and cleaned the basement. Mr. and Mrs. Wilson stayed in the kitchen all afternoon. He cooked spaghetti for dinner, and she baked apple pies for dessert.

The Wilsons finished all their work at six o'clock. Their house looked beautiful inside and out!

The Wilsons' guests arrived at about 7:30. After they arrived, they all sat in the living room. They ate cheese and crackers, drank wine, and talked. Some people talked about their children. Other people talked about the weather. And EVERYBODY talked about how beautiful the Wilsons' house looked inside and out!

The Wilsons served dinner in the dining room at 9:00. Everybody enjoyed the meal very much. They liked Mr. Wilson's spaghetti and they "loved" Mrs. Wilson's apple pie. In fact, everybody asked for seconds.

After dinner everybody sat in the living room again. First, Bob Wilson played the piano and his sister, Margaret, sang. Then, Mr. and Mrs. Wilson showed slides of their trip to Hawaii. After that, they turned on the stereo and everybody danced.

As you can see, the Wilsons' guests enjoyed the party very much. In fact, nobody wanted to go home!

✔ CHECK-UP

Answer These Questions

Answer using full sentences.

1. When did the guests arrive?
2. Where did the guests sit after they arrived?
3. What did they eat and drink before dinner?
4. What time did the Wilsons serve dinner?
5. What did Margaret do after dinner?

Listening

Listen and choose the word you hear.

1.	a.	study	b.	studied
2.	a.	work	b.	worked
3.	a.	stay	b.	stayed
4.	a.	plant	b.	planted
5.	a.	invite	b.	invited
6.	a.	drink	b.	drank
7.	a.	sit	b.	sat
8.	a.	finish	b.	finished
9.	a.	cook	b.	cooked
10.	a.	eat	b.	ate
11.	a.	watch	b.	watched
12.	a.	clean	b.	cleaned

✏ IN YOUR OWN WORDS

For Writing and Discussion

A PARTY

Tell about a party you enjoyed.

What did you eat?
What did you drink?
What did people do at the party?
    (eat, dance, talk about . . .)

Past Tense:
Yes/No Questions
WH Questions
More Irregular Verbs

Late for Work

MARIA GOMEZ

Maria Gomez was born in Peru. She grew up in a small village. She began school when she was six years old. She went to elementary school, but she didn't go to high school. Her family was very poor, and she had to go to work when she was thirteen years old. She worked on an assembly line in a shoe factory.

When Maria was seventeen years old, her family moved to the United States. First they lived in Los Angeles, and then they moved to San Francisco. When Maria arrived in the United States, she wasn't very happy. She missed her friends back in Peru, and she didn't speak one word of English. She began to study English at night, and she worked in a factory during the day.

Maria studied very hard, and now she speaks English well. She's still studying at night, but now she's studying typing. She wants to be a secretary.

Maria still misses her friends back home. But she's very happy now, and she's looking forward to her future in her new country.

✔CHECK-UP

Listening

Listen and choose the best answer based on the story.

1. a. In Peru.
   b. Maria Gomez.

2. a. When I was six years old.
   b. In a small village.

3. a. In a shoe factory.
   b. My family was very poor.

4. a. I wasn't very happy.
   b. We lived in Los Angeles.

5. a. Very hard.
   b. Typing.

IN YOUR OWN WORDS

For Writing and Discussion

Tell a story about yourself or someone in your family. In your story, answer questions such as:

Where were you born?
Where did you grow up?
Where did you go to school?
What did you study?
When did you move? Where?

Like to
Review of Tenses:
Simple Present
Simple Past
Indirect Object Pronouns

**Very Good Friends:
East and West**

**Very Good Friends:
North and South**

VERY GOOD FRIENDS: EAST AND WEST

Tom and Janet are very good friends. They grew up together, they went to high school together, and they went to college together. Now Tom lives in San Diego, and Janet lives in Philadelphia. Even though they live far apart, they're still very good friends.

They write to each other very often. He writes her letters about life on the West Coast, and she writes him letters about life on the East Coast. They never forget each other's birthdays. Last year he sent her a silver bracelet, and she sent him a silk necktie. Tom and Janet help each other very often. Last year he lent her money when she was in the hospital, and she gave him advice when he lost his job.

Tom and Janet like each other very much. They were always very good friends, and they still are.

VERY GOOD FRIENDS: NORTH AND SOUTH

Walter and Linda are our very good friends. For many years we went to church together, we took vacations together, and our children played together. Now Walter and Linda live in Alabama, and we still live here in Minnesota. Even though we live far apart, we're still very good friends.

We write to each other very often. We write them letters about life up north, and they write us letters about life down south. We never forget each other's anniversaries. Last year we sent them a plant, and they sent us a painting. We also help each other very often. Last year we lent them money when they bought a new car, and they gave us advice when we sold our house and moved into an apartment.

We like each other very much. We were always good friends, and we still are.

CHECK-UP

True or False?

1. Tom and Janet are in college.
2. Tom lives on the West Coast.
3. Janet was sick last year.
4. Janet sent Tom a silver bracelet last year.
5. They were friends when they were children.

6. Walter and Linda don't live in Minnesota now.
7. Alabama is in the north.
8. Minnesota and Alabama are far apart.
9. Walter and Linda bought a new car last year.
10. Even though Walter and Linda live far apart from each other, they're still very good friends.

Choose

What word *doesn't* belong?

1. a. grandmother   b. boyfriend   c. girlfriend   d. daughter
2. a. sweater   b. necktie   c. belt   d. doll
3. a. east   b. north   c. coast   d. south
4. a. morning   b. night   c. weekend   d. afternoon
5. a. last year   b. tomorrow morning   c. three years ago   d. yesterday

Listening

Listen and choose the best answer.

1. a. I like to cook spaghetti.
   b. I'm going to cook spaghetti.

2. a. I gave him a watch.
   b. I'm going to give him a necktie.

3. a. Yesterday afternoon.
   b. Tomorrow morning.

4. a. I went skiing.
   b. I go skiing.

5. a. They went to Rome.
   b. They're going to Miami.

6. a. They wrote every week.
   b. They write every week.

7. a. He sent her flowers.
   b. He sends her candy.

8. a. Last weekend.
   b. Tomorrow morning.

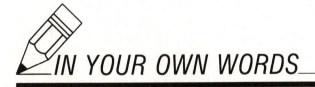

IN YOUR OWN WORDS

For Writing and Discussion

A VERY GOOD FRIEND

Do you have a very good friend who lives far away?   Tell about your friendship.

How do you know each other?
How often do you write to/call each other?
What do you write about/talk about?
Do you send each other presents?
Do you help each other?   How?

69

Count/Non-Count Nouns

Two Bags of Groceries

Delicious!

Tastes Terrible!

TWO BAGS OF GROCERIES

Henry is at the supermarket and he's really upset.   He just bought some groceries, and he can't believe he just spent forty dollars!   He bought only a few oranges, a few apples, a little milk, a little ice cream, and a few eggs.

He also bought just a little coffee, a few onions, a few bananas, a little rice, a little cheese, and a few lemons.   He didn't buy very much fish, he didn't buy very many grapes, and he didn't buy very much meat.

Henry just spent forty dollars, but he's walking out of the supermarket with only two bags of groceries.   No wonder he's upset!

✔ CHECK-UP

Q & A

Using these models, make questions and answers based on the story.

A.   How many *oranges* did he buy?
B.   He bought only a few *oranges*.

A.   How much *milk* did he buy?
B.   He bought only a little *milk*.

How about YOU?

What did YOU buy the last time you went to the supermarket?

(I bought a few . . . /a little . . .)

Listening

Listen and choose what the people are talking about.

1.   a.   ice cream   b.   cookies
2.   a.   chicken   b.   potatoes
3.   a.   meatballs   b.   orange juice
4.   a.   cake   b.   bananas
5.   a.   eggs   b.   butter
6.   a.   salad   b.   french fries
7.   a.   apples   b.   rice
8.   a.   lemonade   b.   lemons

READING

DELICIOUS!

Peter likes chocolate chip cookies. In fact, he eats them all the time. His friends often tell him that he eats too many chocolate chip cookies, but Peter doesn't think so. He thinks they're delicious.

Gloria likes coffee. In fact, she drinks it all the time. Her doctor often tells her that she drinks too much coffee, but Gloria doesn't think so. She thinks it's delicious.

TASTES TERRIBLE!

Sally doesn't like vegetables. In fact, she never eats them. Her parents often tell her that vegetables are good for her, but Sally doesn't care. She thinks they taste terrible.

Michael doesn't like yogurt. In fact, he never eats it. His daughter often tells him that yogurt is good for him, but Michael doesn't care. He thinks it tastes terrible.

IN YOUR OWN WORDS

For Writing and Discussion

Tell about foods you like.

What foods do you think are delicious?
How often do you eat them?
Are they good for you or are they bad for you?
Do you think you eat too many or too much of them?

Tell about foods you don't like.

What foods do you think taste terrible?
How often do you eat them?
Are they good for you or are they bad for you?

Partitives
Count/Non-Count Nouns

Nothing to Eat for Dinner

At The Continental Restaurant

READING

NOTHING TO EAT FOR DINNER

Joan had to work overtime at the office today. She got home late, and she was hungry. When she opened the refrigerator, she was very upset. There was nothing to eat for dinner. Joan sat down and wrote a shopping list. She needed a head of lettuce, a bunch of bananas, a quart of milk, a dozen eggs, two pounds of tomatoes, a pound of butter, two bunches of carrots, and a loaf of bread.

Joan rushed out of the house and drove to the supermarket. When she got there, she was very disappointed. There wasn't any lettuce. There weren't any bananas. There wasn't any milk. There weren't any eggs. There weren't any tomatoes. There wasn't any butter. There weren't any carrots, and there wasn't any bread.

Joan was tired and upset. In fact, she was so tired and upset that she lost her appetite, drove home, didn't have dinner, and went to bed.

✔ CHECK-UP

Q & A

Joan is at the supermarket. Using these models, create dialogs based on the story.

A. Excuse me. I'm looking for a *head of lettuce*.
B. Sorry. There isn't any more *lettuce*.
A. There isn't?
B. No, there isn't. Sorry.

A. Excuse me. I'm looking for a *bunch of bananas*.
B. Sorry. There aren't any more *bananas*.
A. There aren't?
B. No, there aren't. Sorry.

Listening

Listen and choose what the people are talking about.

1. a. milk   b. cheese
2. a. bread   b. flour
3. a. carrots   b. lettuce
4. a. onions   b. butter

5. a. eggs   b. milk
6. a. beans   b. rice
7. a. cake   b. oranges
8. a. cereal   b. soda

READING

AT THE CONTINENTAL RESTAURANT

Yesterday was Sherman and Dorothy Johnson's twenty-third wedding anniversary. They went to the Continental Restaurant for dinner. This restaurant is a very special place for Sherman and Dorothy because they went there on their first date twenty-four years ago.

Sherman and Dorothy sat at a quiet, romantic table in the corner. They had two glasses of wine, and then they ordered dinner. First, Dorothy ordered a bowl of vegetable soup, and Sherman ordered a glass of tomato juice. For the main course, Dorothy ordered baked chicken with rice, and Sherman ordered broiled fish with potatoes. For dessert, Dorothy ordered a piece of apple pie, and Sherman ordered a bowl of strawberries.

Sherman and Dorothy enjoyed their dinner very much. The soup was delicious, and the tomato juice was fresh. The chicken was wonderful, and the rice was tasty. The fish was fantastic, and the potatoes were excellent. The apple pie was magnificent, and the strawberries were out of this world.

Sherman and Dorothy had a wonderful evening at the Continental Restaurant. It was a very special anniversary.

✔ CHECK-UP

Q & A

1. **Sherman and Dorothy are at the Continental Restaurant. They're ordering dinner from their waiter or waitress. Using these lines to begin, create a dialog based on the story.**

   A. Would you like to order now?
   B. Yes. I'd like . . .

2. **The waiter or waitress is asking about the dinner. Using this model, create dialogs based on the story.**

   A. How *is the vegetable soup?*
   B. *It's delicious!*
   A. I'm glad you like *it.*

How about YOU?

Tell about the last time you went to a restaurant:

Where did you go? What did you order?
How was the food? How much did you spend?

77

Future Tense: Will
Might

I Can't Wait for Spring to Come!

Just in Case

I CAN'T WAIT FOR SPRING TO COME!

I'm tired of winter. I'm tired of the snow, I'm tired of cold weather, and I'm sick and tired of winter coats and boots! Just think . . . in a few more weeks it won't be winter any more. It'll be spring. The weather won't be cold. It'll be warm. It won't snow any more. It'll be sunny. I won't have to stay indoors any more. I'll go outside and play with my friends. We'll ride bicycles and play baseball again.

In a few more weeks our neighborhood won't look sad and gray any more. The flowers will bloom, and the trees will become green again. My family will spend more time outdoors. My father will work in the yard. He'll cut the grass and paint the fence. My mother will work in the yard, too. She'll buy new flowers and plant them in the garden. On weekends we won't just sit in the living room and watch TV. We'll go for walks in the park, and we'll have picnics on Sunday afternoons.

I can't wait for spring to come! Hurry, spring!

✔CHECK-UP

True, False, or Maybe?

Answer True, False, or Maybe (if the answer isn't in the story).

1. It's spring.
2. The boy in the story likes to stay inside during the spring.
3. The boy has a cold.
4. The trees aren't green now.
5. The park is near their house.
6. The boy plays baseball with his friends all year.
7. The family has a TV in their living room.
8. The boy's family doesn't like the winter.

How about YOU?

What's your favorite season? Spring? Summer? Fall? Winter? What's the weather like in your favorite season? What do you like to do?

JUST IN CASE

Larry didn't go to work today, and he might not go to work tomorrow either. He might see his doctor instead. He's feeling absolutely terrible, and he thinks he might have pneumonia. Larry isn't positive, but he doesn't want to take any chances. He thinks it might be a good idea for him to see his doctor . . . just in case.

Mrs. Randall didn't go to the office today, and she might not go to the office tomorrow either. She might go to the doctor instead. She feels nauseous every morning, and she thinks she might be pregnant. Mrs. Randall isn't positive, but she doesn't want to take any chances. She thinks it might be a good idea for her to go to the doctor . . . just in case.

Tommy and Julie Harris didn't go to school today, and they might not go to school tomorrow either. They might stay home in bed instead. They have little red spots all over their arms and legs. Mr. and Mrs. Harris think their children might have the measles. They aren't positive, but they don't want to take any chances. They think it might be a good idea for Tommy and Julie to stay home in bed . . . just in case.

✔ CHECK-UP

Choose

Larry is "calling in sick." Choose the correct words and then practice the conversation.

A. Hello. This is Larry. I $\boxed{\begin{array}{c}\text{might}\\\text{can't}\end{array}}^1$ come to work today. I think I $\boxed{\begin{array}{c}\text{will}\\\text{might}\end{array}}^2$ have pneumonia.

B. That's too bad. $\boxed{\begin{array}{c}\text{Are you}\\\text{Will you}\end{array}}^3$ going to see your doctor?

A. I'm not sure. I think I $\boxed{\begin{array}{c}\text{might}\\\text{will}\end{array}}^4$.

B. $\boxed{\begin{array}{c}\text{Not}\\\text{Will}\end{array}}^5$ you be at work tomorrow?

A. I'm not sure. I $\boxed{\begin{array}{c}\text{might not}\\\text{might}\end{array}}^6$ go to work tomorrow either.

B. Well, I hope you feel better soon.

A. Thanks.

Listening

I. Mrs. Harris is calling Tommy and Julie's school.   Listen and choose the correct lines for Mrs. Harris.

1. a. Hello.   This is Mrs. Harris.
   b. Hello.   This is the Park Elementary School.

2. a. I can't.
   b. Tommy and Julie won't be in school today.

3. a. They might have the measles.
   b. Yes.   This is their mother.

4. a. They aren't bad.   They're just sick.
   b. Yes.

5. a. Thank you.
   b. It might be a good idea.

II. Choose the word you hear.

1.	a.	will	b.	we'll	5.	a.	hurt	b.	hit
2.	a.	won't	b.	want to	6.	a.	I'll	b.	I
3.	a.	here	b.	there	7.	a.	wet	b.	red
4.	a.	they	b.	they'll	8.	a.	sick	b.	seasick

IN YOUR OWN WORDS

For Writing and Discussion

You didn't go to work or school today, and you might not go tomorrow either.   Write a note to your boss or teacher and explain why.   (A friend will deliver the note for you.)

```
                              _____, 19 ____

   Dear _____,

        I'm sorry I didn't come to _____ today.
   I'm feeling ........................................................................

   ................................................................................................

   ................................................................................................

        I'll return to _____ very soon.   I hope
   you understand.

                              Sincerely,


                              _____
```

22

Comparatives
Should

Brownsville

It Isn't Easy Being a Teenager

It Isn't Easy Being Parents

READING

BROWNSVILLE

The Taylor family lived in Brownsville for many years.   And for many years, Brownsville was a very good place to live. The streets were clean.   The parks were safe.   The bus system was reliable, and the schools were good.

But Brownsville changed.   Today the streets aren't as clean as they used to be. The parks aren't as safe as they used to be. The bus system isn't as reliable as it used to be, and the schools aren't as good as they used to be.

Because of the changes in Brownsville, the Taylor family moved to Newport last year.   In Newport the streets are cleaner. The parks are safer.   The bus system is more reliable, and the schools are better.   The Taylors are happy in Newport, but they were happier in Brownsville.   Although Newport has cleaner streets, safer parks, a more reliable bus system, and better schools, Brownsville has friendlier people. They're nicer, more polite, and more hospitable than the people in Newport.

The Taylors miss Brownsville.   Even though they're now living in Newport, Brownsville will always be their real home.

✔ CHECK-UP

Q & A

The people of Brownsville are calling Mayor Brown's radio talk show.   They're upset about Brownsville's streets, parks, bus system, and schools.   Using this model and the story, call Mayor Brown.

A.   This is Mayor Brown.   You're on the air.
B.   Mayor Brown, I'm very upset about the *streets* here in Brownsville.
A.   Why?
B.   *They aren't* as *clean* as *they* used to be.
A.   Do you really think so?
B.   Definitely!   You know . . . they say the *streets* in Newport *are cleaner.*
A.   I'll see what I can do.   Thank you for calling.

IT ISN'T EASY BEING A TEENAGER

I try to be a good son, but no matter how hard I try, my parents never seem to be satisfied. They think I should eat healthier food, I should wear nicer clothes, and I should get better grades. And according to them, my hair should be shorter, my room should be neater, and my friends should be more polite when they come to visit.

You know . . . it isn't easy being a teenager.

IT ISN'T EASY BEING PARENTS

We try to be good parents, but no matter how hard we try, our children never seem to be satisfied. They think we should wear more fashionable clothes, we should buy a faster car, and we should listen to more interesting music. And according to them, we should be more sympathetic when they talk about their problems, we should be friendlier when their friends come to visit, and we should be more understanding when they come home late from a Saturday night date.

You know . . . it isn't easy being parents.

✓ CHECK-UP

Choose

What word *doesn't* belong?

1.	a.	sympathetic	b.	fancy	c.	understanding	d.	friendly
2.	a.	clean	b.	convenient	c.	soft	d.	safe
3.	a.	honest	b.	intelligent	c.	reliable	d.	lazy
4.	a.	large	b.	capable	c.	intelligent	d.	talented
5.	a.	friendly	b.	useful	c.	hospitable	d.	polite

Listening

Listen and choose what the people are talking about.

1.	a.	hair	b.	room	4.	a.	car	b.	earring
2.	a.	tennis racket	b.	car	5.	a.	grades	b.	schools
3.	a.	friends	b.	clothes	6.	a.	TV	b.	motorcycle

THE NICEST PERSON

Mr. and Mrs. Jackson are very proud of their daughter, Linda. She's a very nice person. She's friendly, she's polite, she's smart, and she's talented. She's also very pretty.

Mr. and Mrs. Jackson's friends and neighbors always compliment them about Linda. They say she's the nicest person they know. According to them, she's the friendliest, the most polite, the smartest, and the most talented girl in the neighborhood. They also think she's the prettiest.

Mr. and Mrs. Jackson agree. They think Linda is a wonderful girl, and they're proud to say she's their daughter.

THE MOST OBNOXIOUS DOG

Mr. and Mrs. Hubbard are very embarrassed by their dog, Rex. He's a very obnoxious dog. He's noisy, he's stubborn, he's lazy, and he's mean. He's also very ugly.

Mr. and Mrs. Hubbard's friends and neighbors always complain about Rex. They say he's the most obnoxious dog they know. According to them, he's the noisiest, the most stubborn, the laziest, and the meanest dog in the neighborhood. They also think he's the ugliest.

Mr. and Mrs. Hubbard agree. They think Rex is a miserable dog, and they're ashamed to say he's theirs.

✔ CHECK-UP

Q & A

The neighbors are talking. Using these models, create dialogs based on the stories.

A. You know . . . I think Linda is very *nice*.
B. I agree. She the *nicest* girl in the neighborhood.

A. You know . . . I think Rex is very *obnoxious*.
B. You're right. He's the *most obnoxious* dog in the neighborhood.

How about YOU?

Tell about the nicest person you know.

BOB'S BARGAIN DEPARTMENT STORE

Bob's Bargain Department Store is the cheapest store in town. However, even though it's the cheapest, it isn't the most popular. People don't shop there very often because the products are bad. In fact, some people say the products there are the worst in town.

The furniture isn't very comfortable, the clothes aren't very fashionable, the appliances aren't very dependable, and the record players and tape recorders aren't very good. Besides that, the location isn't very convenient, and the salespeople aren't very helpful.

That's why people don't often shop at Bob's Bargain Department Store, even though it's the cheapest store in town.

THE LORD AND LADY DEPARTMENT STORE

The Lord and Lady Department Store sells very good products. In fact, some people say the products there are the best in town.

They sell the most comfortable furniture, the most fashionable clothes, the most dependable appliances, and the best record players and tape recorders. And besides that, their location is the most convenient, and their salespeople are the most helpful in town.

However, even though the Lord and Lady Department Store is the best store in town, people don't often shop there because it's also the most expensive.

HAROLD NEVER GOT THERE

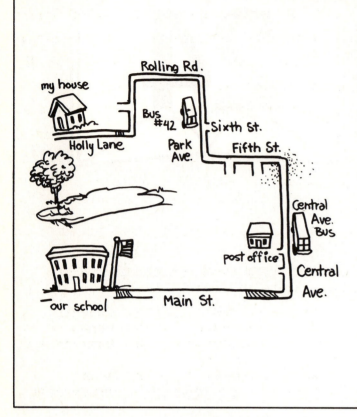

Directions to my house

1. From our school, walk along Main St. to Central Ave. and turn left.
2. Walk up Central Ave. 2 blocks, and you'll see a bus stop at the corner, in front of the post office.
3. Take the Central Ave. bus and get off at Fifth St.
4. Turn left and walk along Fifth St. 3 blocks to Park Ave. and turn right.
5. Walk up Park Ave. 1 block, and you'll see a bus stop at the corner of Park Ave. and Sixth St.
6. Take Bus #42 and get off at Rolling Rd.
7. Turn left and walk along Rolling Rd. 1 block.
8. Turn left again, and walk 2 blocks to Holly Lane and turn right.
9. Walk along Holly Lane. My house is the last one on the right.

Harold had a very difficult time last night. All the other students in his English class went to a party at their teacher's house, but Harold never got there. He followed his teacher's directions, but he made one little mistake.

From their school, he walked along Main Street to Central Avenue and turned left. He walked up Central Avenue two blocks to the bus stop at the corner, in front of the post office. He took the Central Avenue bus and got off at Fifth Street. He turned left and walked along Fifth Street three blocks to Park Avenue and turned right. He walked up Park Avenue one block to the bus stop at the corner of Park Avenue and Sixth Street.

He took Bus Number 42, but he got off at the wrong stop. He got off at River Road instead of Rolling Road. He turned left and walked along River Road one block. He turned left again and walked two blocks, turned right, and got completely lost.

Harold was very upset. He really wanted to go to the party last night, and he can't believe he made such a stupid mistake.

True or False?

1. Harold's English teacher lives on Holly Lane.
2. The Central Avenue bus stops in front of the post office.
3. The teacher made one little mistake in the directions.
4. Harold took the wrong bus.
5. Bus Number 42 goes to Rolling Road.
6. Harold didn't really want to go to the party last night.

What's the Word?

It's very easy to get _____ the zoo from here. Walk up this street _____ the corner and turn right. Walk two blocks and you'll see a bus stop _____ the corner _____ Grove Street and Fourth Avenue. Take the West Side bus and get _____ _____ Park Road. You'll see the zoo _____ the left. It's next _____ the library and across _____ the museum.

Listening

I. Listen and choose the word you hear.

1. a. right   b. left
2. a. down   b. up
3. a. down   b. along
4. a. to   b. on
5. a. of   b. off
6. a. on   b. at

II. Where is the conversation taking place? Listen and choose.

1. a. pet shop   b. cafeteria
2. a. restaurant   b. library
3. a. department store b. laundromat
4. a. hospital   b. hotel
5. a. beauty parlor   b. supermarket

✏ IN YOUR OWN WORDS

For Writing and Discussion

You're going to invite people to your home. Draw a map and write directions to help them get there. (Give them directions from your school.)

✔CHECK-UP

Choose

1. If Ronald _____ go to bed early, he'll be tired in the morning.
   a. doesn't
   b. won't

2. His boss might fire him if _____ late for work.
   a. he'll be
   b. he's

3. Barbara _____ a lot of money if she buys a new car.
   a. spends
   b. will spend

4. If Barbara _____ pay the rent, her landlord might evict her.
   a. can't
   b. won't

5. If Mr. and Mrs. Watson move, they _____ see their family very often.
   a. don't
   b. won't

6. The Watsons won't feel lonely if they _____ move.
   a. don't
   b. might not

Complete These Sentences

1. If I stay up late tonight, . . .
2. If it rains tomorrow, . . .
3. If I'm not busy on Saturday, . . .

4. If the weather is nice on Sunday, . . .
5. If I don't practice English, . . .

Listening

Listen and choose the best answer to complete the sentence.

1. a. he'll be tired tomorrow.
   b. he'll be early in the future.

2. a. her boss might fire her.
   b. her landlord might evict her.

3. a. their grandchildren will move to New Jersey.
   b. their grandchildren will be far away.

4. a. my teacher will be happy.
   b. my teacher won't be happy.

5. a. he won't go back to school.
   b. he'll go back to school.

6. a. his train won't arrive on time.
   b. he might lose his job.

IN YOUR OWN WORDS

For Writing and Discussion

Tell about something you want to do but you know you shouldn't. For example:

"I want to stop studying English."
"I want to move to _____."
"I want to buy an expensive _____."

TOO BAD

I want to _____, but I know I shouldn't. If _____, _____.
If _____, _____. If . . .
_____.
_____.
So, even though I want to _____, I'm not going to. Too bad!

98

26

Past Continuous Tense
Reflexive Pronouns
While-Clauses

A Robbery

Friday the 13th

An Accident

What's the Word?

1. She spilled the _____.
   a. juice   b. children   c. dog
2. I lost my _____.
   a. park   b. accident   c. purse
3. He poked himself in the _____.
   a. gray hair   b. eye   c. glasses
4. They tripped and _____.
   a. dropped   b. fell   c. shaved
5. I was slicing a _____.
   a. flat tire   b. cut   c. banana
6. What a _____!
   a. sorry   b. bad   c. pity

Listening

Listen to the conversations. What happened to these people? Listen and choose the best answer.

1. a. He cut himself.
   b. He looked at himself.
2. a. She tripped.
   b. She got a flat tire.
3. a. They hurt themselves in the basement.
   b. They fell down in the yard.
4. a. He burned himself.
   b. He fainted.
5. a. Somebody stole his wallet.
   b. He got paint on his pants.

READING

AN ACCIDENT

I saw an accident this morning while I was standing at the corner of Elm Street and Central Avenue. A woman in a small red sports car was driving very quickly down Elm Street. A man in a large green truck was driving along Central Avenue very slowly. While he was driving through the intersection, the woman in the red sports car didn't stop at a stop sign and she crashed into the truck. Fortunately, the woman wasn't hurt, but her nose was bleeding a little. The man in the truck wasn't hurt at all. He was shouting at the lady. I left when the police came. I'm glad nobody was hurt very badly.

✔ CHECK-UP

True, False, or Maybe?

Answer True, False, or Maybe (if the answer isn't in the story).

1. The accident took place at the corner of Elm Street and Central Avenue.
2. The woman was driving a small green sports car.
3. The truck driver is always very careful.
4. The truck crashed into the sports car.
5. The woman didn't see the stop sign.
6. The police came after the accident.
7. The woman was tired.

How about YOU?

Tell about an accident you saw: Where were you? What happened? Was anybody hurt?

Could
Be Able to

Mrs. Murphy's Students Couldn't Do Their Homework

The Bathroom Pipe Is Broken

The Television Is Broken

Count/Non-Count Nouns

Carol's Apple Cake

Paul's Beef Stew

Pronoun Review

Trouble with Cars

TROUBLE WITH CARS

It might seem hard to believe, but my friends and I are all having trouble with our cars. There's something wrong with all of them!

Charlie is having trouble with his. The brakes don't work. He tried to fix them by himself, but he wasn't able to, since he doesn't know anything about cars. Finally, he took the car to his mechanic. The mechanic charged him a lot of money, and the brakes STILL don't work! Charlie is really annoyed. He's having a lot of trouble with his car, and he can't find anybody who can help him.

Betty is having trouble with hers. It doesn't start in the morning. She tried to fix it by herself, but she wasn't able to, since she doesn't know anything about cars. Finally, she took the car to her mechanic. The mechanic charged her a lot of money, and the car STILL doesn't start in the morning! Betty is really annoyed. She's having a lot of trouble with her car, and she can't find anybody who can help her.

Mark and Nancy are having trouble with theirs. The steering wheel doesn't turn. They tried to fix it by themselves, but they weren't able to, since they don't know anything about cars. Finally, they took the car to their mechanic. The mechanic charged them a lot of money, and the steering wheel STILL doesn't turn! Mark and Nancy are really annoyed. They're having a lot of trouble with their car, and they can't find anybody who can help them.

I'm having trouble with mine, too. The windows don't go up and down. I tried to fix them by myself, but I wasn't able to, since I don't know anything about cars. Finally, I took the car to my mechanic. The mechanic charged me a lot of money, and the windows STILL don't go up and down! I'm really annoyed. I'm having a lot of trouble with my car, and I can't find anybody who can help me.

✓ CHECK-UP

What's the Word?

1. Charlie tried to fix _____ car by _____.
2. Mark and Nancy's mechanic charged _____ a lot and still didn't fix _____ car.
3. Betty can't find anybody to help _____ fix _____ car.
4. I'm having trouble with _____ car, too. _____ starts in the morning, but the windows are broken.
5. The windows don't go up and down. I tried to fix _____ by _____, but I couldn't.
6. My friends and I can't fix _____ cars by _____ and we're all very angry at _____ mechanics.

Listening

I. Listen and choose the word you hear.

1. a. him   b. her
2. a. him   b. them
3. a. yours   b. hers
4. a. yourself   b. yourselves
5. a. them   b. him
6. a. our   b. her

II. Listen and choose what the people are talking about.

1. a. stove   b. sink
2. a. refrigerator   b. stove
3. a. stereo   b. piano
4. a. camera   b. umbrella
5. a. dog   b. neighbor

How about YOU?

Are you "handy"? Do you like to fix things? Tell about something you fixed. What was the problem? How did you fix it? Also, tell about something you COULDN'T fix. What was the problem? What did you do?

Tape Scripts for Listening Exercises

Chapter 1 – p. 3

Listen and choose the best answer.

1. A. What's your name?
   B. Susan Miller.
2. A. What's your address?
   B. Three ninety-four Main Street.
3. A. What's your apartment number?
   B. Nine D.
4. A. What's your telephone number?
   B. Seven four eight – two two six oh.
5. A. What's your Social Security number?
   B. Oh six oh – eight three – eight two seven five.

Chapter 2 – p. 7

Listen and choose the best answer.

1. Mr. Jones is in the park.
2. Betty is in the library.
3. He's in the kitchen.
4. She's in the living room.
5. They're in the yard.
6. We're in the basement.

Chapter 3 – p. 11

Listen and choose the best answer.

1. What are you doing?
2. What's Mr. Smith doing?
3. What's Mrs. Larson doing?
4. What are Bill and Mary doing?
5. What are you and Henry doing?
6. What am I drinking?

Chapter 4 – p. 15

Listen and choose the best answer.

1. What are you painting?
2. What are you playing?
3. What are they reading?
4. What is she eating?
5. What is he washing?
6. What are you watching?

Chapter 5 – p. 19

Listen and choose the best answer.

1. How's the weather?
2. Tell me about your hotel.
3. How are the children?
4. Tell me about your boyfriend.
5. Tell me about your new apartment.
6. How's your new car?

Chapter 6 – p. 24

Listen to the sentence. Are the people quiet or noisy?

1. They're listening to loud music.
2. I'm reading.
3. She's sleeping.
4. The band is playing.
5. Everybody is singing and dancing.
6. He's studying.

Chapter 7 – p. 28

What words do you hear?

Ex.: My neighborhood is very nice. There's a park nearby, and there's a drug store around the corner.
1. My neighborhood is very convenient. There's a bank around the corner and a restaurant across the street.
2. My neighborhood is very noisy. There's a gas station next to my building, and there's a police station across the street.
3. The sidewalks in my neighborhood are very busy. There's a school across the street and a department store around the corner.
4. There's a big shopping mall outside my city. There's a toy store and a movie theater in the mall.
5. There are many small stores in the center of my town. There's a bakery, a shoe store, and a clothing store.

Chapter 8 – p. 31

Listen and choose the word you hear.

1. These ties are plain.
2. This jacket is dirty.
3. Excuse me. I'm looking for a cotton blouse.
4. I'm wearing my new socks.
5. Is this your boot?
6. Purple umbrellas are very popular.

Chapter 9 – p. 35

Listen and choose the best answer.

1. What does she read?
2. What does she eat?
3. What do they watch?
4. What do they wash?
5. What do you sing?
6. What do you drink?

Chapter 10 – p. 39

Choose the best answer to finish the sentence.

1. A. Do I speak English very well?
   B. Yes, . . .
2. A. Does Mr. Miller live in Toronto?
   B. No, . . .
3. A. Does your brother work in New York?
   B. Yes, . . .
4. A. Do you and your wife clean the house together?
   B. Yes, . . .
5. A. Do your neighbors work in their garden?
   B. No, . . .
6. A. Does your grandmother talk about life back in "the old country"?
   B. Yes, . . .
7. A. Do you go to school on the weekend?
   B. No, . . .
8. A. Does she live in this neighborhood?
   B. No, . . .

Chapter 11 – p. 43

Who and what are they talking about?

1. A. How often do you see her?
   B. I see her every day.
2. A. How often do you wash them?
   B. I wash them every year.
3. A. Do you write to him very often?
   B. Yes. I write to him every week.
4. A. Is it broken?
   B. Yes. He's fixing it now.
5. A. I see them all the time.
   B. That's nice.
6. A. I rarely visit him.
   B. Oh, really?

Chapter 12 – p. 46

Listen and choose the best answer.

1. What are you doing?
2. What does the secretary do?
3. What is the receptionist doing?
4. Is he angry?
5. What do you do when you're sick?

Chapter 14 – p. 51

I. Listen and circle.

1. I can speak English.
2. He can't swim.
3. They can't ski.
4. She can play the piano.
5. We can dance.
6. I can't type.

II. Choose what each person can do.

1. I can sing. I can't dance.
2. He can't file. He can type.
3. She can't fix motors. She can repair locks.
4. He can cook. He can't bake.
5. I can drive a truck. I can't drive a bus.
6. She can't teach history. She can teach science.

Chapter 14 – p. 56

Listen and choose the words you hear.

1. A. When are you going to visit me?
   B. Next month.
2. A. When are you going to begin your vacation?
   B. This Sunday.
3. A. When is your son going to call my daughter?
   B. This afternoon.
4. A. When are your neighbors going to move?
   B. Next November.
5. A. When is she going to get her driver's license?
   B. Next week.
6. A. When are you going to do your laundry?
   B. This evening.
7. A. When are we going to go to the concert?
   B. This Thursday.
8. A. When is your daughter going to finish college?
   B. Next winter.
9. A. When are you going to buy a car?
   B. Tomorrow.
10. A. When is the landlord going to fix the window?
    B. At once.

Chapter 15 – p. 61

Listen and choose the word you hear.

1. I studied at the library all day.
2. We work at the restaurant all day.
3. They stayed home all afternoon.
4. I plant flowers in my garden in the spring.
5. They invited their friends to their parties.
6. Mr. and Mrs. Franklin drink lemonade all summer.
7. Tim and Bill sat in their living room all morning.
8. They finish their work at four o'clock.
9. Mr. Wilson cooked dinner for his family.
10. The people at the party ate cheese and crackers.
11. She watched TV in the living room.
12. He cleaned the basement every day.

Chapter 16 – p. 64

Listen and write the missing words.

Shirley enjoyed her day off yesterday. She got up late, went jogging in the park, took a long shower, and ate a big breakfast. In the afternoon, she went to the movies with her sister, and in the evening, she had dinner with her parents. After dinner they sat in the living room and talked. Shirley had a very pleasant day off yesterday.

Chapter 17 – p. 66

Listen and choose the best answer based on the story.

1. Maria, where were you born?
2. When did you begin school?
3. Why did you go to work when you were thirteen?
4. How did you feel when you arrived in the United States?
5. What are you studying now?

Chapter 18 – p. 69

Listen and choose the best answer.

1. What are you going to cook tomorrow?
2. What did you give your husband for his birthday?
3. When did you plant these flowers?
4. What do you do in the winter?
5. Where did your parents go on their vacation?
6. How often do they write to each other?
7. What did he send her?
8. When are you going to move?

Chapter 19 – p. 72

Listen and choose what the people are talking about.

1. A. How much do you want?
   B. Just a little, please.
2. A. Do you want some more?
   B. Okay. But just a few.
3. A. These are delicious!
   B. I'm glad you like them.
4. A. I ate too many.
   B. How many did you eat?
5. A. They're bad for my health.
   B. Really?
6. A. It's very good.
   B. Thank you.
7. A. Would you care for some more?
   B. Yes, but not too much.
8. A. There isn't any.
   B. There isn't?!

Chapter 20 – p. 76

Listen and choose what the people are talking about.

1. A. How much does a pound cost?
   B. A dollar forty.
2. A. How many loaves do we need?
   B. Three.
3. A. They're very expensive this week.
   B. You're right.
4. A. Sorry. There isn't any more.
   B. There isn't?
5. A. I need two quarts.
   B. Okay.
6. A. I bought too many.
   B. Really?
7. A. There weren't any in the refrigerator.
   B. Who ate them?
8. A. How much does the large box cost?
   B. Two nineteen.

Chapter 21 – p. 82

I. Mrs. Harris is calling Tommy and Julie's school. Listen and choose the correct lines for Mrs. Harris.

1. Hello. Park Elementary School.
2. Yes, Mrs. Harris. What can I do for you?
3. Oh? What's the matter?
4. That's too bad. Are you going to take them to the doctor?
5. Well, I hope Tommy and Julie feel better soon.

II. Choose the word you hear.

1. We'll be ready in half an hour.
2. I want to come to work today.
3. Don't smoke in here!
4. They'll work in their yard every Saturday.
5. Don't stand there! You might get hurt!
6. I call the doctor when I'm sick.
7. Careful! There are wet spots on the floor.
8. I'm sick and tired of sailing.

Chapter 22 – p. 85

Listen and choose what the people are talking about.

1. A. I think it should be shorter.
   B. But it's very short now!
2. A. I like it. It's fast.
   B. It is. It's much faster than my old one.
3. A. Why can't they be more polite?
   B. It isn't easy.
4. A. Is it reliable?
   B. Yes, but it isn't as reliable as my old one.
5. A. They aren't as good as they were last time.
   B. Don't worry. They'll be better next time.
6. A. Which one should I buy?
   B. Buy this one. It's more powerful than that one.

Chapter 23 – p. 90

Listen and choose the best answers to complete the commercial.

1. Good news for shoppers everywhere! Franklin's Department Store is having a big sale this week. Everything is on sale, and our products are very . . .
2. Our products are also better than items at other stores. Our clothes are more . . .
3. Our appliances are more . . .
4. And everybody agrees our salespeople are more . . .
5. Come on down to Franklin's Department Store! Don't shop at those other stores! We're the . . .

Chapter 24 – p. 93

I. Listen and choose the word you hear.

1. The school is on the right, next to the post office.
2. Walk up Town Road to Park Street.
3. Drive along Fourth Avenue to Station Street.
4. Take the subway to Bond Street.
5. The bus stop is at the corner of Main and fifth.
6. Take this bus and get off at Rolling road.

II. Where is the conversation taking place? Listen and choose.

1. A. Please give me an order of chicken.
   B. An order of chicken? Certainly.
2. A. Shh! Please be quiet! People are reading.
   B. Sorry.
3. A. Do you want to buy these clothes?
   B. Yes, please.
4. A. Can I visit my wife?
   B. Yes. She and the baby are in Room 407.
5. A. How much does one head cost?
   B. Seventy-nine cents.

Chapter 25 – p. 98

Listen and choose the best answer to complete the sentence.

1. If Ronald stays up late tonight . . .
3. If Barbara doesn't have enough money to pay the rent . . .
3. If the Watsons move to Arizona . . .
4. If I do my homework carelessly . . .
5. If Johnny doesn't feel better tomorrow . . .
6. If he doesn't translate accurately . . .

Chapter 26 – p. 102

Listen to the conversations. What happened to these people? Listen and choose the best answer.

1. A. How did you do that?
   B. I did it while I was shaving.
2. A. When did it happen?
   B. While I was getting off a bus.
3. A. What were they doing?
   B. They were playing outside.
4. A. Why do you think it happened?
   B. It was a very hot day.
5. A. The park isn't as safe as it used to be.
   B. I agree.

Chapter 27 – p. 104

Listen and choose the best answer.

1. I couldn't sit down.
2. We couldn't see the sun.
3. Did she enjoy the hamburger?
4. He wasn't able to lift it.
5. Why weren't the plumbers able to fix it?

Chapter 28 – p. 108

Listen and choose the best words to complete the sentences.

1. This tastes terrible. I used too much . . .
2. You know . . . the next time you bake this, you should try to use fewer . . .
3. You're a little too heavy. You must eat less . . .
4. This pie is delicious! I can't believe it has so many . . .
5. This tastes better than it did the last time I made it. I think it's because I used fewer . . .
6. Remember, we couldn't finish everything the last time we ate here. This time let's order less . . .

Chapter 29 – p. 111

Listen and choose the best answer.

1. When will we be arriving in Tokyo?
2. When will they be getting married?
3. How late did you work last night?
4. How much longer will the pies be baking?
5. Will they be leaving soon?
6. When will the boss be retiring?

Chapter 30 – p. 115

I. Listen and choose the word you hear.

1. Do you know him well?
2. Did you see them today?
3. Yours will be ready at five o'clock.
4. Careful! You might hurt yourselves!
5. I'll be glad to help him.
6. We're having trouble with her car.

II. Listen and choose what the people are talking about.

1. I'm going to have to call the plumber.
2. It's broken. It won't get cold.
3. She plays very well.
4. Careful! It's raining. Don't let it get wet!
5. He parked in the yard all night.

Index

A

A few, 72
A little, 72
Able to, 105
Adjectives, 18-19, 30-31, 88-90
   comparative of, 84-85, 90
   superlative of, 88-90
Adverbs, 96
   comparative of, 96
   of frequency, 42-43
As + adjective + as, 84

C

Can/can't, 50-53
Clothing, 31
Colors, 31
Comparative:
   of adjectives, 84-85, 90
   of adverbs, 96
Could/couldn't, 104-105
Count/non-count nouns, 72-73, 76, 108

D

Directions, 92-93

F

Fewer, 108

G

Going to + verb, 56-58

H

Had to, 104
Have to, 52-53

I

If, 97-98
Indirect object pronouns, 68-69

L

Less, 108

M

Might, 81-82
Months, 57-58

N

Nationalities, 6
Nouns:
   count/non-count, 108
   singular/plural, 30-31

O

Object pronouns, 42-43

P

Partitives, 77
Plural, 30-31
Possessive adjectives, 14-15
Possessive pronouns, 114-115
Prepositions of location, 26-28
Pronouns:
   indirect object, 68-69
   object, 42-43
   possessive, 114-115
   reflexive, 101
   review of, 114-115

Q

Quantity:
   a few, 72
   a little, 72
   fewer, 108
   less, 108

R

Reflexive pronouns, 101

S

Should, 85
Singular/plural, 30-31
Superlatives, 88-90

T

Tenses:
   future continuous, 110-111
   future: going to, 56-58
   future: will, 80
   past continuous, 100-102
   present continuous, 10-11, 14-15, 18-19, 22-24
   review of tenses, 68-69
   simple past, 60-61, 64, 66
   simple present, 34-36, 38-40
   simple present vs. present continuous, 46-47
There is/there are, 26-28
Time expressions, 56, 110-111
To Be:
   past tense, 66
   present tense, 2-3, 6-7, 18-19
Too + adverb, 96

W

While-clauses, 101-102